Raspberry Pi Camera Controls
For Windows and Debian-Linux using Pyth
Python language, runs on most operating syster

First Edition

Herb Norbom

Author of:
Raspberry Pi Robot with Camera and Sound
Robot Wireless Control Made Simple with Python and C
Python Version 2.6 Introduction using IDLE
Python Version 2.7 Introduction using IDLE
Python Version 3.2 Introduction using IDLE and PythonWin
Bootloader Source Code for ATMega168 using STK500 For Microsoft Windows
Bootloader Source Code for ATMega168 using STK500 For Debian-Linux
Bootloader Source Code for ATMega328P using STK500 For Microsoft Windows
Bootloader Source Code for ATMega328P using STK500 For Debian-Linux
Books Available on Amazon and CreateSpace

Where we are aware of a trademark that name has been printed with a Capital Letter.

Great care has been taken to provide accurate information, by both the author and the publisher, no expressed or implied warranty of any kind is given. No liability is assumed for any damages in connection with any information provided.

Copyright © 2013 Herb Norbom
All rights reserved.
ISBN-13:978-1493713714
ISBN-10: 149371371X

Table of Contents

FOREWARD...3
PREFACE...3
   Why Python?..3
PROCESS STEPS..4
   Supplies and Devices..4
   Work Directories-Raspberry Pi...4
   Setup Windows PC..5
   Setup Debian-Linux PC...5
   Program or Text Editor..5
   Python Start...5
   Testing the Pi Camera...8
   Pi Camera Module...11
      class Camera...12
      class UpdateVideoDisplay..12
      class UpdateOptionDisplay..12
      class UpdateVideoOptionDisplay..12
      setupTK(frMain)...12
      viewPicture...13
      startV...13
      cameraSTILLandVIDEOfinal2.py..14
      Remote VIDEO on Windows PC..29
THE END OR THE BEGINNING..30
APPENDIX..30
   Summary for Raspberry Pi Setup..30
   Simple DOS commands..31
   logging on to the Pi from Windows..32
   logging on to the Pi from Debian-Linux...32
   Starting Netcat and MPlayer Windows...33
   starting Netcat and MPlayer Debian-Linux..33
   PuTTY for Windows...34
   PuTTY for Debian-Linux..35
   Xming X Server for Windows...35
   Geany for Windows...36
   Geany for Raspberry Pi...36
   Netcat for Raspberry Pi and Debian-Linux...36
   Netcat for Windows..36
   Debian-Linux Shell Scripts...36
   Debian-Linux Commands...37
Reference Sites..39
   Raspberry..39
   Raspberry - Camera...39
   Xming...39
   Python..39
   Tkinter..40
   Linux..40

FOREWARD

The Raspberry Pi is a wonderful computer. It is small and supported by a growing base of users. The Pi's small price and small footprint make it very suitable for a variety of applications. As additional hardware is made available I expect the Pi's popularity to grow. One of the recent additions to the Pi accessories is the Pi's Camera. This is small device that interfaces directly with the Pi. With the Pi's support of WiFi one can quickly visualize many applications.

PREFACE

This book grew out of my desire to appeal to people who wanted to use the Pi Camera but were not interested in the robotics application. While much of the information contained in my book Raspberry Pi Robot with Camera and Sound is included here I have expanded and focused on the Camera portion in this book. I am going to include in this book what we need to accomplish in order to operate the Camera from a remote PC running Windows or Debian-Linux; or if you just want to run the Camera from your Pi. We will write a Camera control program using Python. If you are building a robot consider the complete book and you will be able to add this program to your robot if you so desire.

As a point of reference I am currently running Microsoft Windows XP Professional Version 2002 Service Pack 3 on a Dell Dimension PC with Pentium4 CPU 3.00GHz. I am also running Debian Release 6.0.7 (squeeze) on an old PC with an Intel(R) Pentium(R) 4 CPU 2.40GHz. The Kernel Linux is 2.6.32-5-686. I am also using the GNOME Desktop 2.30.2 using the bash shell. The Raspberry Pi is running Linux Raspbian, Kernel 3.6.11, version wheezy, built from 2013-09-25-wheezy-raspbian.zip, and the Debian-Linux version is 7.2. We will use the installed Python 2.7 software. My home network utilizes a Netgear router.

So to get started I have listed the steps we will go through. As far as setting up the Raspberry Pi I am not going to go very far into that, but I do provide a summary in the Appendix. There are excellent sources on line, no use building a new wheel. But get the biggest SD card you can. The 4 GB just will work, but bigger is better. At this point my Pi disk is consuming less than 2 GB.

While we are going to setup the Raspberry Pi to be operational without a monitor, keyboard or mouse I suggest that as you are learning and testing that you leave those items connected.

Why Python?

Even If you have never programmed before, I suggest you start with Python. We are going to be using a lot of Python. While I am sure everyone has their own favorite programming language and good reasons for it, at this point Python is my choice. As you learn Python you will gain insight into areas you are going to need to control your robot. There are several reasons for choosing Python, they include the following:
- Object Oriented – will flow with events rather than straight lines
- Not compiled, uses an interpreter – therefore, quick results while developing applications
- Runs on Windows, Linux, Unix, even Apple – it is portable
- There is lot of FREE information on the web about it
- Python is free and already installed on your Raspberry Pi
- There are a lot of free modules - you may need to enhance your project
- What you learn, program flow and structure will to some extent carry over to C, C++ or C#, or whatever language you evolve to
- Python has a good built-in GUI, Tkinter

Yes, of course there are disadvantages, if you are going to do something for resale Python may not be the language for you. If you are here, you are probably not close to having anything to sell, so don't worry about that. Just because Python uses an interpreter do not think you are limited in terms of program size and complexity. The Raspberry Pi has multiple versions of Python installed. As of this time Python 2.7.3 is the default version. We are going to use the default version vs. Python 3 which is also installed. We are going to write our programs on the Raspberry Pi and when finished we will be able to operate our Pi Camera from either a Windows PC or a Debian-Linux PC or from the Pi console. If you are not familiar with Python at all consider the book 'Python Version 2.7 Introduction using IDLE' sold on Amazon, yes I am the author, sorry about the self promoting. While I am going to provide the complete source code I am not going to go into the same depth in explaining the code as I did in my first book 'Robot Wireless Control Made Simple with Python and C'. If you are interested you can search Amazon using my name for a complete list of books.

PROCESS STEPS

- Of course you need the Raspberry Pi and various hardware items listed under Supplies and Devices. You will need to get the Pi working over a wireless communication.

- You are going to be downloading software, if you do not have a high speed connection this is going to be very difficult.

- You need to setup your directories, just makes life easier.

- We will write our Programs using Python 2.7 as that is installed on the Raspberry Pi and it is an excellent choice anyway. Also 'Tkinter' is installed with this version of Python.

Supplies and Devices

The following parts list can be viewed as a starting point, substitute as you like. The Raspberry Pi is sold by a number of distributors. Prices shown are what I paid and they will probably have changed.

Part	Possible Source	Source Part #	Min Qty	Approx. Price	Ext. Price
Raspberry Pi Model B 512MB	AdaFruit	ID: 998	1	39.95	39.95
5V Micro USB AC Adapter	MCM	28-13060	1	6.61	6.61
Wireless N NANO USB Adapter 802.11b	MCM	831-2761	1	14.99	14.99
Raspberry Pi Camera Board	AdaFruit	ID: 805	1	29.95	29.95
Desktop High Speed USB2.0 Hub with Power Supply	Find best one. Need while testing.	Check for one working with Raspberry	1		
SD Memory Card(min4GB)	AdaFruit	many choices available	1		
SD Memory Card Reader/Writer	Find best one	very possible your computer has one	1		

I did not include a monitor, keyboard or mouse, hopefully you have spares to use while you get everything running; it is possible to run the Pi without them. We will not need them once all is working and that includes the USB Hub. For the Raspberry items in particular check out the package deals that are available. While I have used these suppliers I am not saying they are the best or the least expensive. I am not affiliated with any of them.

Work Directories-Raspberry Pi

We are going to be writing a number of programs and it can get very confusing where they are located. Also from a backup view point it is nice to have them in a separate directory. I suggest you make a separate directory now. I called my directory 'CAMERA' in the Pi home directory.

Setup Windows PC

For our remote control we are going to need some software on the PC. There are a number of options but I am just going to list what I was able to get working. You are going to need PuTTY and Xming. PuTTY provides the communication link and Xming provides the X11 capabilities for our PC. What we are going to do is have our Raspberry Pi running and then from our Windows PC log on to the Raspberry Pi. See the Appendix for downloading PuTTY and for setup. Xming is also covered in the Appendix. With everything working we will log on to the Raspberry Pi using "pi".

Setup Debian-Linux PC

If you are going to run your Pi Camera from Debian-Linux you will need to add software to the Raspberry Pi as well as to your Debian-Linux PC. While just logging in to the Pi is easy, running a GUI is a little more difficult. From a Terminal prompt on the Debian-Linux PC enter the following command:

$ ssh -X 192.168.1.9 -l pi   You will need to have enabled ssh on the Pi.

Change the IP address to match where your Pi is connected. Note the capital X and the small letter L in front of pi. See the Appendix for an illustration.

Whether you are using Debian-Linux or Windows you can run your Pi 'headless' (without a monitor). It is easier to set everything up with the Pi having a monitor, keyboard and mouse. In the Appendix I provide information and illustrations for the setup process.

Program or Text Editor

I am going to install Geany on my Raspberry Pi, on my Windows PC and on the Debian-Linux PC, see the Appendix for installation information. You can use any text editor you like, that includes Python's Idle, nano, vi or vim or whatever you like. Each has pluses and minuses. A very nice feature of Geany is that you can run the program right from Geany. Once you are running the program remotely or as they say 'headless' with no monitor attached you may appreciate this feature.

Python Start

The following walks you through your first Python program using a Windows PC. The process for running from Debian-Linux is similar to the Windows process. See the Appendix for getting this working. Once you are logged onto the Pi from either the Windows PC or the Debian-Linux PC the process becomes the same because you are running from the Pi.

First let us make a very small Python program. I have installed Geany on the Raspberry Pi and I have logged onto the Raspberry Pi from my Windows PC using PuTTY, log-in as pi. I have Xming running on the PC at this point. I suggest you change to our CAMERA directory. Enter from the $ prompt 'cd /home/pi/CAMERA' or if in the pi home directory.

Before we write our first program script I suggest you type 'python' at the # prompt. If all is well you should get a message from Python. Mine says Python 2.7.3 (default, Jan 13, 2013....) and gives the Python prompt of >>>.

If you get the Python prompt you can enter "Crtl z" to exit Python and return to the # prompt.

Illustration 1

With Python working let us write our first script using Geany. (You will need to have Xming working, see Appendix for that installation.) Enter 'geany' at the # prompt. Go ahead and enter the program code and save file as 'firstTK.py'. The 'py' extension is required by Python and Geany also uses it to identify the script type.

Illustration 2

One of the many nice things about Geany is that you can execute the script without leaving Geany. First let us make sure that the execute command in Geany is correct. Click on 'Build' and select 'Set Build Commands'. Under the last items on the screen you should see Execute as python "%f". That is the only command we are interested in at this point. (The "%f" is your program name that Geany enters automatically for you.)

Illustration 3

Click OK or Cancel to close the window. To run the Python script, click on the Execute button. A LXTerminal window will open and our Tkinter window will be open on it.

Illustration 4

Our Tkinter window also shows.

This works like a normal window, click on the x to close. When you close the Tkinter window the LXTerminal window will prompt you with the message "Press return to continue", the LXTerminal closes when you press return.

If you had problems with this you may want to try running directly from your Raspberry Pi console. We need to have this working before proceeding. If you can, take some time and explore the features of Geany. If you want to run from the Pi console you can just know that Geany needs to have X windows running. If you are running from Gnome or LXDE you may see Geany on the menu. If not there select LXTerminal and run from that window by typing geany.

I am sure you are aware, but just in case I need to mention how to shutdown your Pi. You should always run a 'shutdown' procedure. These procedures ensure an orderly closing of files and help prevent corruption of your SD. A good procedure is "shutdown -h now", if not logged in as root, precede the command with "sudo". On the Pi Gnome Desktop GUI there is a shutdown icon.

Testing the Pi Camera

We can do some simple commands from the terminal prompt to ensure that the camera is working. The first one will be to see if the Pi Camera help is available. I will be running the examples from my Windows PC. I am using PuTTY and Xming.

Enter   "raspivid -?"   (Note in all the commands for the camera spacing is important.)

```
pi@raspberrypi ~/CAMERA $ raspivid -?
Display camera output to display, and optionally saves an H264 capture at reques
ted bitrate


usage: raspivid [options]

Image parameter commands

-?, --help       : This help information
-w, --width      : Set image width <size>. Default 1920
-h, --height     : Set image height <size>. Default 1080
-b, --bitrate    : Set bitrate. Use bits per second (e.g. 10MBits/s would be -b 1
0000000)
-o, --output     : Output filename <filename> (to write to stdout, use '-o -')
-v, --verbose    : Output verbose information during run
-t, --timeout    : Time (in ms) to capture for. If not specified, set to 5s. Zero
 to disable
-d, --demo       : Run a demo mode (cycle through range of camera options, no cap
ture)
-fps, --framerate    : Specify the frames per second to record
-e, --penc       : Display preview image *after* encoding (shows compression arti
facts)
-g, --intra      : Specify the intra refresh period (key frame rate/GoP size)

Preview parameter commands

-p, --preview    : Preview window settings <'x,y,w,h'>
-f, --fullscreen     : Fullscreen preview mode
-op, --opacity   : Preview window opacity (0-255)
-n, --nopreview  : Do not display a preview window
```

Illustration 5

```
Image parameter commands

-sh, --sharpness     : Set image sharpness (-100 to 100)
-co, --contrast      : Set image contrast (-100 to 100)
-br, --brightness    : Set image brightness (0 to 100)
-sa, --saturation    : Set image saturation (-100 to 100)
-ISO, --ISO          : Set capture ISO
-vs, --vstab         : Turn on video stablisation
-ev, --ev            : Set EV compensation
-ex, --exposure      : Set exposure mode (see Notes)
-awb, --awb          : Set AWB mode (see Notes)
-ifx, --imxfx        : Set image effect (see Notes)
-cfx, --colfx        : Set colour effect (U:V)
-mm, --metering      : Set metering mode (see Notes)
-rot, --rotation     : Set image rotation (0-359)
-hf, --hflip         : Set horizontal flip
-vf, --vflip         : Set vertical flip
-roi, --roi          : Set region of interest (x,y,w,d as normalised coordinates [0.0-1.0])

Notes

Exposure mode options :
off,auto,night,nightpreview,backlight,spotlight,sports,snow,beach,verylong,fixedfps,antishake,fireworks

AWB mode options :
off,auto,sun,cloud,shade,tungsten,fluorescent,incandescent,flash,horizon

Image Effect mode options :
none,negative,solarise,sketch,denoise,emboss,oilpaint,hatch,gpen,pastel,watercolour,film,blur,saturation,colourswap,washedout,posterise,colourpoint,colourbalance,cartoon

Metering Mode options :
average,spot,backlit,matrix

pi@raspberrypi ~/CAMERA $
```

Illustration 6

With this working let's try the commands to display a picture and then a short video. To display a picture on the console enter the following: "raspistill -w 400 -h 400". On occasion the console will start displaying improper characters. If that happens you can enter "reset" at the prompt. Let's try a short video display on the console. At the terminal prompt enter "raspivid -w 400 – h 400". Both commands are shown in the following illustration.

```
pi@raspberrypi ~/CAMERA $ raspistill -w 400 -h 400
pi@raspberrypi ~/CAMERA $ raspivid -w 400 -h 400
pi@raspberrypi ~/CAMERA $
```

Illustration 7

You can play with entering the various options show from the Help command given earlier. While entering commands from the prompt or from a script file works, I wanted more. I wanted a program that could control the camera. Make changes on the fly to make a video or take a still picture; configure the various options; and save pictures or videos. With these goals in mind I wrote the following program that I hope is not too convoluted. I had planned to provide two programs, one for video and one for still pictures. As I went through the development it became clear that the majority of the options applied to both types. So for better or worse one program it is. While I do like to develop applications in modules I did not find that to be of benefit here, you may feel differently as the program is getting a little on the long side.

Pi Camera Module

The goal of this module is to have camera defaults set and to be able to adjust the settings from our Python program. In some of my other books I go into more depth on some of the standard modules we will be using, but there is a wealth of information on the web also. If you happened to have followed my book "Raspberry Pi Robot with Camera and Sound" you will quickly see that this program is based on the camera module included in that book. This program has a great many more options. In fact I have tried to include as many as I thought applicable. The program is driven by the options that you select. Your first decision is to select the picture type, STILL or VIDEO. From there you can make your selections in any order you like. The Pi Camera has lots of options that are fun to play with in combinations. To help visualize the program the following illustration shows the control window.

Illustration 8

The framing or groupings on the window are primarily driven by the type of choices each offers. Where the choice is only VIDEO I have put that in a separate frame. As you get into the program you will hopefully note and maybe even agree that I have used variable names that are intuitive to the process. I have tried to place comments in the program to help me to remember and you to see what I am trying to accomplish.

class Camera

After all the imports are coded I set up our first class, the class Camera. We will create two instances of the class one for display and one to work with. This method makes it a little easier to update the display when changes are made to our variables. We will have two instances of the class Camera: SELF and DISP. I have used the same values in setting up both instances

class UpdateVideoDisplay

We are also going to create a class for UpdateVideoDisplay. In this class we use labels and buttons for making desired changes. Within this class I have setup a FRAME, you can see Illustration 8 the text is 'Setup1'. Within this class we also setup a function 'def videoChange(DISP)' to update the Labels of our display. We call this function when we want to update our display. Following this class I have added the functions that are called when a variable is changed.

class UpdateOptionDisplay

This class UpdateOptionDisplay is used to contain the items that I used an "OptionMenu" to offer the valid choices. You will note I have tried to include all the available options for each item. On Illustration8 you can see the Frame text as 'Setup2', I called the Frame 'combFr' as it will hold this class and the next one.

class UpdateVideoOptionDisplay

The class UpdateVideoOptionDisplay is used to control VIDEO only options. The control and updating procedure is the same type used for our first class. The items for the display and option choices are included in the Frame name 'Setup2'. After the Labels and variable displays the functions that are called are shown.

setupTK(frMain)

Because I want this program to run as an import or independently we use the "if __name__=='__main__':" procedure. If you run the program from a prompt or directly from Geany the program 'knows' to execute the 'main' and the items below it. If we call the program, after importing it, we will call a function of the program. If you are not familiar with this I hope the fog lifts as you work through the program. When you run from the prompt the program will of course do it's normal checking and setup, but it will run the function setupTk(1) as its first step. I have set a switch to indicate where the program is being run from, if run independently I want to set up a normal Tk() window, you may think of it as the root or master window. If run or import from a separate program I want to make the window a Toplevel window; as I do not want to have two master or root windows running.

I have added a Frame to keep our Buttons organized. Most of the Buttons are standard buttons, you click them and they call a function and run accordingly. The exception is the Button which I have set equal to B1. This button determines if you are selecting a VIDEO or STILL camera action. When you click the button a function is called like the other Buttons. Within the function some interesting items are looked at. The function looks at what the 'text' of the button is set at and changes to the opposite. If if was VIDEO it will change to STILL. This took me a fair amount of time to get working, but once understood the concept can be applied to any button and its configuration options.

Also included in this section are 'Checkbuttons'. These are just on/off type selections. Yes they are also placed in a Frame, shown on Illustration8 as 'CHECKBOX'.

Near the end of this section the 'combFr is defined, note we use this Frame for two of the classes described earlier.

The last two items are just to run the earlier described functions.

viewPicture

This function is different from the other functions. You can use this to list the 'gif' files in a directory and to view the gif format pictures. As I wanted to stick to standard pictures that Python could display without going obtaining additional modules, only 'gif' formatting is shown. You can look at other Python modules, 'pil' for example for other formats. When you have selected a 'gif' picture it will be displayed on the screen you are running this program from.

startV

This is the function that actually sends the command to the Pi Camera. Needless to say it is the meat of the program. You will probably quickly note that the vertical and horizontal flip options are treated differently than other options. I could not get them to work when I listed them by themselves. So of course I cheated a little. I made a short decision tree and tacked them on to the back of the 'rotation' option as needed. Having a good thing working I continued the 'tacking' on process as needed for visual stabilization, color effect and ISO. While on the subject of ISO, I am not sure how ISO works with the Pi Camera. I could not see any difference when the option was on or off. But what do I know so I left it in the program.

You may have noticed that I have setup STILL pictures to be saved to a file on the Pi Raspberry. After the picture is saved you can view it on your PC or on the Raspberry Pi. For the VIDEO you can stream the video to your PC, view it on the Raspberry Pi OR save it to a file on the Raspberry Pi. The video format needs to be 'h264' format. To view the video file on the Raspberry Pi you can run 'omxplayer' from a Pi terminal prompt. If you want to copy the file to your PC I suggest you use a USB drive, NetCat, Samba or other file transfer utility. You can also setup to save the VIDEO on your Pi. Be aware if saving the VIDEO file on your Raspberry Pi that the files can get quite large very quickly.

The actual command sent to the Pi Camera depends on your selection of STILL or VIDEO. For STILL I use the subprocess Popen and have set the process equal to 'p'. I can then obtain the 'pid' and tell the process to wait until finished.

For VIDEO the process is very similar to the STILL process with the exception of NOT including the 'wait' instruction. Leave it off so you can click on the 'STOP VIDEO' button shown in Illustration7.

For VIDEO I define the port or file that you want to send the video to. (You will need to have downloaded Netcat for the Raspberry Pi and the Windows or Linux-Debian PC that you plan to use as your control. You will also need to use a video player on the machine you want to display the video on. I am using MPlayer, see appendix for notes on installing that as well and Netcat.) Note the spacing of the commands and the line continuation character '\'. If you have been playing with the camera you may have had some problems stopping the video. As we are using the subprocess function to start the camera we can easily capture its 'pid', (process identifier). Once we have that we can issue a 'kill' command to stop the process.

If you are running the program from the Raspberry Pi console the video will display on the console, and you will not need Netcat or MPlayer for that purpose. But once we start running remotely you will need them.

When you get to the point of running the program, you will need to start the Netcat program on your PC first. You will see this running in your DOS or command prompt window. Getting Netcat and the MPlayer software running takes some time. You will at some point notice a very noticeable lag between what the camera sees and what is displayed on your screen. This is a result of writing to the cache and reading from the cache. The procedure uses a first in first out from the cache. Try just a short run with the camera on, click stop video, let the cache empty then restart the video. I hope that you get decent results; my delays went away doing this.

The following screen shots are the complete Python program for controlling your Pi Camera. I generally like to give the reader the chance to build the program in blocks so that the debugging process is a little easier. The program works fine, but you will find that spacing is critical. This program did not lend itself to that practice. As you look at the code you may want to try to break down the process into creating the 'classes' one at a time. A lot of the code you enter can be copied, pasted and then edited to save a few keystrokes. Whichever way you go the following is the code. You can of course use whatever name you like for the program, just use the 'py' extension.

cameraSTILLandVIDEOfinal2.py

```
# Control Program for Raspberry Pi camera
# using Python 2.7.3   setup to run on Linux
# author Herb   11/7/2013 company RyMax, Inc. www.rymax.biz
# for personal hobby use only, include references to RyMax Inc. for
# resale or commercial use contact RyMax, Inc. for written persmission.
from Tkinter import *
from tkFileDialog import askopenfilename
import tkSimpleDialog
import os
import subprocess
import signal

class Camera:
    def __init__(DATA,picType,width,height,sharpness,contrast,brightness,
        saturation,evCompensation,pictureName,rotation,sTime,
        vBitrate,vTime,vFps,vPort):
        DATA.picType=picType
        DATA.width=width
        DATA.height=height
        DATA.sharpness=sharpness
        DATA.contrast=contrast
        DATA.brightness=brightness
        DATA.saturation=saturation
        DATA.evCompensation=evCompensation
        DATA.pictureName=pictureName
        DATA.rotation=rotation
        DATA.sTime=sTime
        DATA.vBitrate=vBitrate
        DATA.vTime=vTime
        DATA.vFps=vFps
        DATA.vPort=vPort
```

Illustration 9

```
32    SELF = Camera(
33                    "STILL",                    #Picture type will be STILL or VIDEO
34                    600,                        #display width
35                    400,                        #display height
36                    100,                        #sharpness
37                    0,                          #contrast
38                    50,                         #brightness
39                    0,                          #saturation
40                    0,                          #EV Compensation
41                    "picture.gif",              #picture file name
42                    0,                          #rotation
43                    5,                          #still time pause before picture in ms
44                    10000000,                   #video bit rate 10MBits
45                    9999,                       #video time in ms
46                    31,                         #video frames per second
47                    "| nc 192.168.1.4 5001" )   #video default output port for VIDEO
48                                                #remote using NetCat
49    #for DISP setting same as SELF
50    DISP = Camera(  ,600, 400, 100,0,50,0,0,"picture.gif",0,5,
51                    10000000,9999,31,"| nc 192.168.1.4 5001")
52    class UpdateVideoDisplay():
53        def __init__(DISP):
54            DISP.vFr = LabelFrame(TOP, width =40, height=118,
55                bd=2, text= Setup, relief=GROOVE)
56            DISP.vFr.grid(column =0,row=1,sticky=(N,W,S))
57            Label(DISP.vFr, text='***Current Value***').grid(column=0,row=1)
58            Label(DISP.vFr, text='CLICK to CHANGE').grid(column=1,
59                row=1,sticky=(W))
60        #width
61            DISP.width = StringVar()
62            DISP.width.set(SELF.width)
```

Illustration 10

```
63              Label(DISP.vFr,textvariable=DISP.width).grid(column=0,
64                  row=2,sticky=(E))
65              Button(DISP.vFr,text="width",command=imWidth).grid(column=1,
66                  row=2,sticky=(W))
67          #height
68              DISP.height = StringVar()
69              DISP.height.set(SELF.height)
70              Label2=Label(DISP.vFr, textvariable=DISP.height)
71              Label2.grid(column=0, row=3, sticky=(E))
72              Button(DISP.vFr,text="Height",command=imHeight).grid(column=1,
73                  row=3,sticky=(W))
74          #sharpness
75              DISP.sharpness = StringVar()
76              DISP.sharpness.set(SELF.sharpness)
77              Label(DISP.vFr,textvariable=DISP.sharpness).grid(column=0,
78                  row=4,sticky=(E))
79              Button(DISP.vFr,text="Image Sharpness",command=sharpnessSet).grid(
80                  column=1,row=4,sticky=(W))
81          #contrast
82              DISP.contrast = StringVar()
83              DISP.contrast.set(SELF.contrast)
84              Label(DISP.vFr,textvariable=DISP.contrast).grid(column=0,
85                  row=5,sticky=(E))
86              Button(DISP.vFr,text="Image Contrast",command=contrastSet).grid(
87                  column=1,row=5,sticky=(W))
88          #brightness
89              DISP.brightness = StringVar()
90              DISP.brightness.set(SELF.brightness)
91              Label(DISP.vFr,textvariable=DISP.brightness).grid(column=0,
92                  row=6,sticky=(E))
93              Button(DISP.vFr,text="Image brightness",command=brightnessSet).grid(
```

Illustration 11

```
 94                   column=1,row=6,sticky=(W))
 95          #saturation
 96              DISP.saturation = StringVar()
 97              DISP.saturation.set(SELF.saturation)
 98              Label(DISP.vFr,textvariable=DISP.saturation).grid(column=0,
 99                   row=7,sticky=(E))
100              Button(DISP.vFr,text=             ,command=saturationSet).grid(
101                   column=1,row=7,sticky=(W))
102          #evCompensation
103              DISP.evCompensation = StringVar()
104              DISP.evCompensation.set(SELF.evCompensation)
105              Label(DISP.vFr,textvariable=DISP.evCompensation).grid(column=0,
106                   row=8,sticky=(E))
107              Button(DISP.vFr,text=             ,command=evCompensationSet).grid(
108                   column=1,row=8,sticky=(W))
109          #pictureName
110              DISP.pictureName = StringVar()
111              DISP.pictureName.set(SELF.pictureName)
112              Label(DISP.vFr,textvariable=DISP.pictureName).grid(column=0,
113                   row=9,sticky=(E))
114              Button(DISP.vFr,text=             ,
115                   command=pictureNameSelect).grid(column=1,row=9,sticky=(W))
116          #rotation
117              DISP.rotation = StringVar()
118              DISP.rotation.set(SELF.rotation)
119              Label(DISP.vFr,textvariable=DISP.rotation).grid(column=0,
120                   row=10,sticky=(E))
121              Button(DISP.vFr,text=             ,command=rotationSet).grid(
122                   column=1,row=10,sticky=(W))
123          #still time pause
124              DISP.sTime = StringVar()
```

Illustration 12

```
                    DISP.sTime.set(SELF.sTime)
                Label(DISP.vFr,textvariable=DISP.sTime).grid(column=0,
                    row=11,sticky=(E))
                Button(DISP.vFr,text="Still Time Pause",command=sTimeSet).grid(
                    column=1,row=11,sticky=(W))

        def videoChange(DISP):
            DISP.width.set(SELF.width)
            DISP.height.set(SELF.height)
            DISP.contrast.set(SELF.contrast)
            DISP.sharpness.set(SELF.sharpness)
            DISP.brightness.set(SELF.brightness)
            DISP.saturation.set(SELF.saturation)
            DISP.evCompensation.set(SELF.evCompensation)
            DISP.pictureName.set(SELF.pictureName)
            DISP.rotation.set(SELF.rotation)
            DISP.sTime.set(SELF.sTime)

def imWidth():
    temp=tkSimpleDialog.askinteger("Enter integer for width",
        "Between 100 & 1920: ",
        initialvalue=SELF.width,minvalue=100,maxvalue=1920)
    if temp != None:
        SELF.width=temp
    UpdateVideoDisplay()
def imHeight():
    temp=tkSimpleDialog.askinteger("Enter integer for height",
        "Between 50 & 1080: ",
        initialvalue=SELF.height,minvalue=50,maxvalue=1080)
    if temp != None:
        SELF.height=temp
```

Illustration 13

```
156          UpdateVideoDisplay()
157     def sharpnessSet():
158         temp=tkSimpleDialog.askinteger(
159             
160             initialvalue=SELF.sharpness,minvalue=-100,maxvalue=100)
161         if temp != None:
162             SELF.sharpness=temp
163         UpdateVideoDisplay()
164     def contrastSet():
165         temp=tkSimpleDialog.askinteger(
166             
167             initialvalue=SELF.contrast,minvalue=-100,maxvalue=100)
168         if temp != None:
169             SELF.contrast=temp
170         UpdateVideoDisplay()
171     def brightnessSet():
172         temp=tkSimpleDialog.askinteger(
173             
174             initialvalue=SELF.brightness,minvalue=0,maxvalue=100)
175         if temp != None:
176             SELF.brightness=temp
177         UpdateVideoDisplay()
178     def saturationSet():
179         temp=tkSimpleDialog.askinteger(
180             
181             initialvalue=SELF.saturation,minvalue=-100,maxvalue=100)
182         if temp != None:
183             SELF.saturation=temp
184         UpdateVideoDisplay()
185     def evCompensationSet():
186         temp=tkSimpleDialog.askinteger(
```

Illustration 14

```
187                 "Between -10 & 10: ",
188                 initialvalue=SELF.evCompensation,minvalue=-10,maxvalue=10)
189         if temp != None:
190             SELF.evCompensation=temp
191         UpdateVideoDisplay()
192     def pictureNameSelect():
193         temp=tkSimpleDialog.askstring("For STILL Picture File Name",
194                 "Example: myPicture.gif",
195                 initialvalue=SELF.pictureName)
196         if temp != None:
197             SELF.pictureName=temp
198         UpdateVideoDisplay()
199     def rotationSet():
200         temp=tkSimpleDialog.askinteger("Integer for Image Rotation",
201                 "Between 0 & 359: ",
202                 initialvalue=SELF.rotation,minvalue=0,maxvalue=359)
203         if temp != None:
204             SELF.rotation=temp
205         UpdateVideoDisplay()
206     def sTimeSet():
207         temp=tkSimpleDialog.askinteger("Time to Pause before Still Picture",
208                 "Between 0 & 5000: ",
209                 initialvalue=SELF.sTime,minvalue=0,maxvalue=5000)
210         if temp != None:
211             SELF.sTime=temp
212         UpdateVideoDisplay()
213
214 class UpdateOptionDisplay():
215     global exposure, awb, ifx, metering
216     def __init__(DISP):
217         DISP.oFr = LabelFrame(combFr, width =30, height=118,
```

Illustration 15

```
218             bd=2, text=        , relief=GROOVE)
219             DISP.oFr.grid(column =0,row=0,sticky=(N,W,S))
220     #exposure
221         exposure.set(         )
222         Label(DISP.oFr,text=          ).grid(column=1,row=8,sticky=(W))
223         OptionMenu(DISP.oFr,exposure,
224                 ,
225                 ,                       ,).grid(column=0,
226             row=8,sticky=(W))
227     #awb
228         awb.set(      )
229         Label(DISP.oFr,text=      ).grid(column=1,row=9,sticky=(W))
230         option= OptionMenu(DISP.oFr,awb,
231                 ,
232                 ,           ).grid(column=0,row=9, sticky=(W))
233     #ifx
234         ifx.set(       )
235         Label(DISP.oFr,text=             ).grid(column=1,row=10,sticky=(W))
236         option= OptionMenu(DISP.oFr,ifx,
237                 ,
238                 ,
239                 ,
240             )
241         option.config(width=10)
242         option.grid(column=0,row=10, sticky=(W,E))
243     #metering
244         metering.set(       )
245         Label(DISP.oFr,text=         ).grid(column=1,row=11,sticky=(W))
246         option= OptionMenu(DISP.oFr,metering,
247                 ,       ).grid(column=0,row=11, sticky=(W))
248
```

Illustration 16

```python
249  class UpdateVideoOptionDisplay():
250      global exposure, awb, ifx, metering
251      def __init__(DISP):
252          DISP.vFr = LabelFrame(combFr, width =40, height=118,
253          bd=2, text='VIDEO Only Setup', relief=GROOVE)
254          DISP.vFr.grid(column =0,row=1,sticky=(N,W,S,E))
255          #bitrate
256          DISP.vBitrate = StringVar()
257          DISP.vBitrate.set(SELF.vBitrate)
258          Label(DISP.vFr,textvariable=DISP.vBitrate).grid(column=0,
259              row=0,sticky=(E))
260          Button(DISP.vFr,text="BitRate/Second",command=bitrate).grid(column=1,
261              row=0,sticky=(W))
262          #fps
263          DISP.vFps = StringVar()
264          DISP.vFps.set(SELF.vFps)
265          Label(DISP.vFr,textvariable=DISP.vFps).grid(column=0,
266              row=1,sticky=(E))
267          Button(DISP.vFr,text="Frames/Second",command=imfps).grid(column=1,
268              row=1,sticky=(W))
269          #videoTime
270          DISP.vTime = StringVar()
271          DISP.vTime.set(SELF.vTime)
272          Label(DISP.vFr,textvariable=DISP.vTime).grid(column=0,
273              row=2,sticky=(E))
274          Button(DISP.vFr,text="Video Time On",command=vTime).grid(column=1,
275              row=2,sticky=(W))
276          #port
277          DISP.vPort = StringVar()
278          DISP.vPort.set(SELF.vPort)
279          Label(DISP.vFr,textvariable=DISP.vPort).grid(column=0,
```

Illustration 17

```
280                    row=3,sticky=(E))
281              Button(DISP.vFr,text="Port or File",command=portSelect).grid(column=1,
282                    row=3,sticky=(W))
283         def video2Change(DISP):
284              DISP.vBitrate.set(SELF.vBitrate)
285              DISP.vFps.set(SELF.vFps)
286              DISP.vTime.set(SELF.vTime)
287              DISP.vPort.set(SELF.vPort)
288    def bitrate():
289         temp=tkSimpleDialog.askinteger("Enter integer for BitRate",
290              "Example 10,000,000 for 10MBits",initialvalue=SELF.vBitrate)
291         if temp != None:
292              SELF.vBitrate=temp
293         UpdateVideoOptionDisplay()
294    def imfps():
295         temp=tkSimpleDialog.askinteger("Enter integer for fps",
296              "Between 5 & 50",
297              "if you change may need to change hc also",
298              initialvalue=SELF.vFps,minvalue=5,maxvalue=50)
299         if temp != None:
300              SELF.vFps=temp
301         UpdateVideoOptionDisplay()
302    def vTime():
303         temp=tkSimpleDialog.askinteger("Integer for video time ms",
304              "Between 999 & 99999999",
305              initialvalue=SELF.vTime,minvalue=999,maxvalue=99999999)
306         if temp != None:
307              SELF.vTime=temp
308         UpdateVideoOptionDisplay()
309    def portSelect():
310         temp=tkSimpleDialog.askstring("Enter Port or filename.h264",
```

Illustration 18

```python
311                         "Example 192.168.1.6 5001 or video.h264 ,
312                initialvalue=SELF.vPort)
313     if temp != None:
314         SELF.vPort=temp
315     UpdateVideoOptionDisplay()
316
317 def setupTk(frMain):
318     global TOP
319     if frMain==1:              #program run as stand alone
320         TOP = Tk()
321     if frMain==0:              #program imported & run from other Python script
322         TOP = Toplevel()
323     TOP.title( "Camera STILL and VIDEO Picture Controls" )
324     TOP.geometry( "245x90+400+50" ) #width, height, placement x  y
325     bFr=LabelFrame(TOP, width=218, height=50,bd=2, relief=GROOVE)
326     bFr.grid(column=0,row=0,sticky=(N,W,E,S))
327     Button(bFr,text="START CAMERA",fg="green",width=9,command=startV).grid(
328         column=0,row=0,sticky=W)
329     global B1
330     B1=Button(bFr,text=SELF.picType,fg="green",width=3,command=setTYPE)
331     B1.grid(column=1,row=0,sticky=W)
332     Button(bFr,text="Help",fg="brown",command=helpV).grid(column=2,row=0,
333         sticky=W)
334     Button(bFr,text="VIEW PICTURE",fg="black",width=9,command=viewPicture).grid(
335         column=0,row=1,sticky=W)
336     Button(bFr,text="STOP VIDEO",fg="red", command=stopV).grid(column=1,row=1,
337         sticky=W)
338     Button(bFr,text="EXIT", fg="red", command=exitCamera).grid(column=2,row=1,
339         sticky=W)
340 #define Checkbuttons for various items that are on or off
341 #define Frame for Checkbutton
```

Illustration 19

```
342        DISP.cFr = LabelFrame(TOP, width =50, height=50,
343             bd=2, text=           , relief=GROOVE)
344        DISP.cFr.grid(column =1,row=0,sticky=(N,W))
345        global v1, v2, v3,v4,v5
346        v1 = IntVar()
347        v2 = IntVar()
348        v3 = IntVar()
349        v4 = IntVar()
350        v5 = IntVar()
351        C1 = Checkbutton(DISP.cFr,text=           , variable=v1)
352        C1.grid(column=0,row=0,sticky=W)
353        C2 = Checkbutton(DISP.cFr,text=           , variable=v2)
354        C2.grid(column=0,row=1,sticky=W)
355        C3 = Checkbutton(DISP.cFr,text=           , variable=v3)
356        C3.grid(column=0,row=2,sticky=W)
357        C4 = Checkbutton(DISP.cFr,text=           , variable=v4)
358        C4.grid(column=1,row=0,sticky=W)
359        C5 = Checkbutton(DISP.cFr,text=           , variable=v5)
360        C5.grid(column=1,row=1,sticky=W)
361        UpdateVideoDisplay()
362        global exposure, awb, ifx, metering
363        exposure=StringVar()
364        awb=StringVar()
365        ifx=StringVar()
366        metering=StringVar()
367        global combFr   #Frame for holding the frames Setup2 and VIDEO Only Setup
368        combFr = LabelFrame(TOP, width =200, height=118)
369        combFr.grid(column=1, columnspan=3,row=1,sticky=(N,W,S,E))
370        UpdateOptionDisplay()
371        UpdateVideoOptionDisplay()
372
```

Illustration 20

Illustration 21

Illustration 22

```
435         if SELF.picType==' TILL ':
436             camStill =            +str(SELF.width)\
437             +    +str(SELF.height)\
438             +       \
439             +      +str(SELF.sharpness)\
440             +      +str(SELF.contrast)\
441             +      +str(SELF.brightness)\
442             +      +str(SELF.saturation)\
443             +      +str(SELF.evCompensation)\
444             +      +str(pexposure)\
445             +      +str(SELF.sTime)\
446             +      +str(pawb)\
447             +      +str(pifx)\
448             +      +str(pmetering)\
449             +dispSET\
450             +      +str(SELF.pictureName)
451             p = subprocess.Popen(camStill, shell=True, preexec_fn=os.setsid )
452             print
453             print camStill
454             p.wait()         #need to wait until subprocess completes
455         if SELF.picType==       :
456             camVideo =             +str(SELF.width)\
457             +    +str(SELF.height)\
458             +      +str(SELF.sharpness)\
459             +      +str(SELF.contrast)\
460             +      +str(SELF.brightness)\
461             +      +str(SELF.saturation)\
462             +      +str(SELF.evCompensation)\
463             +      +str(SELF.vBitrate)\
464             +      +str(SELF.vTime)\
465             +      +str(SELF.vFps)\
```

Illustration 23

```
466                    +       +str(pexposure)\
467                    +        +str(pawb)\
468                    +        +str(pifx)\
469                    +        +str(pmetering)\
470                    +dispSET\
471                    +        +str(SELF.vPort)
472             p = subprocess.Popen(camVideo, shell=True, preexec_fn=os.setsid )
473             print                 , p.pid
474             print camVideo
475
476     def exitCamera():
477         global p, preexec_fn
478         try:
479             os.killpg(p.pid, signal.SIGTERM)
480         except:
481             pass
482         TOP.destroy()
483     def stopV():
484         global p, preexec_fn
485         os.killpg(p.pid, signal.SIGTERM)
486     def helpV():
487         camStill=
488         subprocess.Popen(camStill, shell=True )
489     if __name__ ==            :
490         setupTk(1)
491         mainloop()
492
```

Illustration 24

Now that you have all the coding done, time to run. IF in Geany select your "CameraSTILLandVIDEOFINAL2.py" and select 'Execute'. Or if you are running from a command prompt enter

"python CameraSTILLandVIDEOFINAL2.py".

Remote VIDEO on Windows PC

On the Windows PC I set up the following bat file to start Netcat and MPlayer. I saved Netcat and MPlayer in My Documents directory. To run them I set up a batch file in the 'netcat' directory. See the Appendix for instructions on downloading Netcat and MPlayer. The following is the simple bat file I created to get it running. You can setup a similar script on the Debian-Linux PC if you like, remember to make it executable if using Debian-Linux.

Illustration 25

THE END OR THE BEGINNING

I hope that you have learned a lot and had some fun.

Visit the web site www.rymax.biz for additional information. I would like to learn from your experience, you can e-mail me at herb@rymax.biz.

APPENDIX

Summary for Raspberry Pi Setup

There is a good chance that the steps taken to setup your Raspberry Pi will evolve over time. The following is just a guide as to the steps that I took. While I did build a new OS for this book, you need to expect things to change, and of course I may have forgotten something, but I don't think so. Check out the web for the latest instructions.

```
Raspberry pi building the SD card
        I have settled on the debian-wheezy with the desktop that is standard with it LXDE
        I have used the pc as the source and a desktop running debian-wheezy -linux
        download the file from
see     http://www.raspberrypi.org/downloads
see     http://elinux.org/RPi_Easy_SD_Card_Setup
        same for either pc on linux
        under file manager double click on the file to unzip    2012-12-16-wheezy-raspbian.zip
Download image  2013-09-25-wheezy-raspian.zip   file 577 Mb  Version wheezy Kernel 3.6  FILE size 605,227,145 on MY PC Disk
        this then is used to generate the image file which is approx 2,892,800 KB
        from Prompt run sha1sum  on the img file   2013-09-25-wheezy-raspian.img  PRIOR TO UNZIPPING
        should get following  Raspberry Pi download page  99e6b5e6b8cfbf66e34437a74022fcf9744ccb1d
        takes a few minuets to run  MAKE SURE YOU RUN ON THE ZIP FILE
        I got 99e6b5e6b8cfbf66e34437a74022fcf9744ccb1d   2013-09-25-wheezy-raspbian.img

Download SD Formatter 4.0  sor SD/SDHC/SDXC
        https://www.sdcard.org/downloads/formatter_4/
        I installed My Documents\SDFormatter  It put Icon on Desktop
Make sure you set FORMAT SIZE ADJUSTMENT to ON in the Options menu
        http://elinux.org/RPi_Hardware_Basic_Setup
Disk Image Win32
        down load from
        http://sourceforge.net/projects/win32diskimager/

Insert SD in Raspberry Pi and power up the Raspberry Pi
        should boot to raspi-config
        select EXPAND-ROOTFS -Expand Root Partion to Fill SD Card  I did not want a separate partition
        then let it reboot  should now be able to see full size
        login  pi
        pwd   raspberry
        sudo raspi-config
        change password for pi
            sudo passwd pi
                enter new password twice
        enable SSH under advanced options
        exit raspi-config
        sudo apt-get update
        sudo apt-get upgrade

        suggest a reboot
        login pi
        sudo raspi-config
           enable camera
        A good idea to run   again
        sudo apt-get update
        sudo apt-get upgrade
        suggest a reboot
        login pi
            if you want to start desktop startx
```

Illustration25A

Simple DOS commands

Before we go any further, a few quick words on DOS commands. They can do damage, they are not very user friendly; they will destroy without asking twice. So make sure the command you enter is the command that you want and that you know what the command is going to do.
Simple DOS commands, execute from the DOS command prompt. Remember DOS is not case sensitive.

- Dir or dir   – This will give you the contents of the current directory
- Help   – all the commands that are available
- Help dir   – gives you all the options available with dir
- cd {dir name}– change directory, you would add the directory name
- cd ../   – moves up the directory tree one level
- cls   –clear the DOS window screen

logging on to the Pi from Windows

Make sure you have started the Xming server. You need to start PuTTY and use the settings shown for PuTTY. You will log-in as 'pi'. PuTTY will display the Pi's log-in window. See the Appendix sections for setting up PuTTY and Xming.

Illustration25B

logging on to the Pi from Debian-Linux

There are a lot of ways to do this, the following is the simplest method I have found to enable a GUI interface, have a video feed and log-in as the user pi. You must have ssh enabled on the Pi. You probably have already set this. You can check by entering on the Pi the following command sudo raspi-config and looking at the Advance Options, A4 and making sure that SSH is enabled.

From a terminal prompt on your Debian-Linux PC enter the command "ssh -X 192.168.1.9 -l pi". As I mentioned earlier make sure you use a capital X and a small letter L. You will be asked for the pi password. As you can see from the Illustration that I changed to our program directory and started Geany.

Illustration 26

As you can see from Illustration26 I did not have the correct IP address the first try. The second time I get an

RSA warning, no not from NSA. Just accept and you will not get the warning the next time. Now that you are logged on to the Raspberry Pi, change directory to CAMERA and you can type geany and select your program and run it.

Starting Netcat and MPlayer Windows

We are only using DOS to start our Netcat program. I am going to create a bat script in the location where my '*cmd*' prompt opened. Adjust the following as needed for your system.

Use a simple text editor, Geany or the DOS edit program to create a simple bat file for starting the video capture. At this point I have downloaded and installed Netcat and MPlayer. In my case both were installed in directories under "My Documents" adjust the bat file or script as needed. But what the script or bat file does is change to the directory where I installed Netcat and issue a list directory command. I then put a second bat file in that directory to actually start Netcat and display the video. While you can combine the two bat files if you like, I kept them separate because I kept playing with the options on the second one and was tired of changing directories. My first bat file is named "raspberryFeed.bat" and it is saved in the directory where the command or DOS prompt opens. It only has two lines, so if you are good at remembering where things are you may not need this bat file. The two lines are:
cd My Documents\Netcat
dir

The second bat file is really the more important one as I will not remember the command to start Netcat. This bat file is named startNETCAT.bat and I saved it in the Netcat directory.(see Illustration25) I just have one line, you can adjust for example fps, but seems to work best if it matches what you set the camera program at. You can also play with the cache size. For Windows this is the command that I use:
nc.exe -L -p 5001 | ..\mplayer-svn-36442\mplayer.exe -fps 31 -cache 2048 -

nc.exe   is the Netcat program
-L   is for Windows only, instructs program Listen harder, or a persistent listener, like NSA
-p 5001   is the local port that I want to listen to
| the vertical line is the pipe command, what Netcat hears we pipe to mplayer.exe
..\mplayer-svn-36442   is the directory that I installed mplayer.exe in
mplayer.exe   is the program that displays the video that Netcat hears
-fps   frames per second
-cache   size (you can play with and try various sizes)
   –   need this last dash to make it work

To end the program use "Ctrl c".

To test you can run the script on the Windows PC. On the Pi you need to start the camera with the command "raspivid -t 9999 -o - | nc 192.168.1.4 5001". Note the IP address is the IP for the Windows PC. A good reference site is: http://www.raspberrypi.org/camera .

starting Netcat and MPlayer Debian-Linux

The start-up is very similar to the Windows version. From a terminal prompt on the Debian-Linux PC I entered the following command which I have saved in a script file. Remember to make your script file executable. That is a small letter L after nc.

Illustration 27

To test you can run the script in Illustration27 on the Debian-Linux PC. On the Pi you need to start the camera with the command "raspivid -t 9999 -o - | nc 192.168.1.6 5001". Note the IP address is the IP for the Debian-Linux PC. A good reference site is: http://www.raspberrypi.org/camera .
Illustration 28 shows a sample of what the output on the Debian-Linux PC looks like.

Illustration 28

PuTTY for Windows

For our communications you will need PuTTY© installed on your PC. The following describes how to obtain the PuTTY executable. Go to the main PuTTY Download Page. http://www.chiark.greenend.org.uk/~sgtatham/putty/download.html. From this page you can select the appropriate file. I suggest you get the Windows installer for everything except PuTTYtel. At this point the latest release is version .63.

Open PuTTY and click on SSH, make appropriate changes. For Host Name or IP address I am using the IP address (for the Pi) and Port 22. Under Category select (Connection SSH X11) and Enable X11 forwarding. Under Category Session you can name your file under Saved Sessions, which is a real good idea. There are lots of options you set, but we are just using PuTTY to setup our Xming communication so our Python program has a GUI interface.

The PuTTY help files should have been included if things are not working.

Illustration 29   *Illustration 30*

PuTTY for Debian-Linux

The install is very straight forward. Just run "sudo apt-get install putty". The PuTTY settings are the same as for the Windows version mentioned above. Nice to have but not needed as we will use the standard ssh included with Debian-Linux.

Xming X Server for Windows

This program is needed on your Windows PC to support the GUI interface for our Python Tkinter items. You can download the software from http://sourceforge.net/projects/xming/ . I tried many options, but I think most of my problem in getting it to work was in my not setting up PuTTY. You will need PuTTY for this to work. After you have downloaded Xming you need to run the XLaunch program. I selected "Multiple windows" and on the next screen I selected "Start no client". On the next screen I have checked the "Clipboard" to Start the integrated clipboard manager. On the next screen I saved the configuration and clicked Finish. The Xming server needs to be running on your PC for our Python Tkinter to work.

Illustration 31   *Illustration 32*

Geany for Windows

The program has many useful features as well as being a very nice text editor. Go to www.geany.org . The geany-1.2.3.1 setup.exe Full Installer is approximately 8Mb.

Geany for Raspberry Pi

Pretty straight forward enter: "sudo apt-get install geany". If you want to install on the Debian-Linux PC the same command works.

Netcat for Raspberry Pi and Debian-Linux

This is a very neat program but expect to get warning as to security. You should evaluate your system and determine if risk justifies reward. In my case I went for it. You need to install this software on the Raspberry Pi and on your PC.

On Raspberry Pi and your Debian-Linux PC if using that the following command.

sudo apt-get install netcat

The program is also available from http://sourceforge.net/projects/nc110/

Netcat for Windows

On Windows try http://nmap.org/download.html#windows there are download instructions and a self installer. Expect security warnings, you need to decide, if you are comfortable. This will get you the binaries; if you want the source it is also available. I installed the Netcat software in the "My Documents" directory. While there are other ways to skin the cat I could at least make this work pretty well.

Debian-Linux Shell Scripts

A few hints for making your scripts executable. Not your Python scripts, Python handles that. You can write your script using any text editor, vi or vim, etc. I

- The file name doesn't need an extension.
- Comments are a line starting with a pound sign '#'
- You need to have permission to execute or run the script. After you have saved your script open a

terminal window and go to the directory where you saved the script. Type 'ls -l filename' for example. (small letter 'L') The permissions will be shown. Something similar to the following table, third row.

position 1	2	3	4	5	6	7	8	9	10
directory flag	User read	User write	User execute	Group read	Group write	Group execute	Other read	Other write	Other execute
-	r	w	-	r	-	-	r	-	-
-	r	w	x	r	-	-	r	-	-

You need to make the script an executable. You can do this from a terminal window be in the directory with your script and type chmod u+x filename. Then retype the ls -l filename and you should see the change as shown on row 4 of the preceding table. (NOTE a small letter L) To run the script from the terminal window, be in the same directory and type. ./filename or type . filename (Notice the . and space)

Debian-Linux Commands

Before using understand that many of the commands have options that are not shown here. For those who may have forgotten some simple Linux commands, a very quick refresher course follows. This is only the tip of the iceberg, just listing a few. Before we go any further, a few quick words on commands. They can do damage, they are not very user friendly; they will destroy without asking twice. So make sure the command you enter is the command that you want and that you know what the command is going to do. Remember when you execute a command that involves a filename you may want to proceed the filename with a "./". Example "cat ./filename".

cat filname	list contents of file
cat filename > filename2	copy filename to filename2
cat /etc/debian_version	this will show what version of Debian you are running
cat /etc/os-release	will show misc. os information
cd	change to home directory
cd /	change to root directory
cd ..	move up one level in the directory tree
chown newower filename	change the owner of filename to the newowner name
chmod u+x filename	example of changing permission of stk500work for the user to execute
clear	clear the screen can also use Ctrl L
cp filename filename2	copy filename to filname2
date	show current day, date and time
df -h	File systems mounted, size, used, avail Use%, where mounted
dmesg	This will show the devices attached, very useful for finding PL2303 and other serial devices attached
echo $SHELL	to see what shell you are running

find -name filename	find the specified filename
free -m	display memory used and free
id	what user you are and what groups you are in
ifconfig	display connections information, (eth0, lo, wlan0, etc)
ip addr show	show connection addresses
kill number	If you need to stop a runaway process, number is the process ID (PID)
lp filename	print filename to default printer
lpstat -t	show default printer
lsusb	list usb devices running on computer
lsusb -v	run as sudo for a complete list, with v is a verbose list
mkdir filename	make a new directory
more filename	list the file, will do in pages
mv filename filname2	move or rename filename to filname2
pwd	to see what your current directory is
whoami	to see what yser you are
ps -p$	generates a process error but shows options
ps -T or ps	show all processes on this terminal
ps -A	show all processes running on computer
ps aux	show all process running on computer, user, PID & more
pstree	show all processes in a tree format
ps -p$$	show current PID TTY TIME CMD
uname -a	display version and kernel
rm filename	delete file specified
reboot	do an immediate shutdown and then reboot
reset	use when console has character map a mess, resets to standard
rmdir directory	remove specified directory
rm -r directory	remove specified directory and contents of the directory
shutdown -h now	shutdown the computer now, you may need sudo in front of command
who	list all users

Reference Sites
The following sites have useful information.

Raspberry

http://www.raspberrypi.org

http://www.element14.com/community/groups/roadtest?ICID=roadtest_subnav

http://www.engadget.com/2012/09/05/cambridge-university-raspberry-pi-guide/

http://www.engadget.com/2012/09/04/raspberry-pi-getting-started-guide-how-to/

http://www.raspberrypi.org/downloads

http://elinux.org/RPiconfig

http://elinux.org/RPi_VerifiedPeripherals

http://elinux.org/RPi_Distributions

http://elinux.org/R-Pi_Troubleshooting

http://elinux.org/RPi_Hardware#Power

http://shallowsky.com/blog/hardware/pi-battery.html

http://elinux.org/RPi_raspi-config

http://asliceofraspberrypi.blogspot.com/2013/05/displaying-system-information-and.html

Raspberry - Camera

http://elinux.org/Rpi_Camera_Module

Xming

http://sourceforge.net/projects/xming/

http://www.straightrunning.com/XmingNotes/pixming.php

Python

www.sourceforge.net
www.docs.python.org
www.astro.ufl.edu
www.sthurlow.com
www.learnpython.org
http://www.astro.ufl.edu/~warner/prog/python.html
www.tutorialspoint.com/python/index.htm
https://developers.google.com/edu/python
http://anh.cs.luc.edu/python/hands-on/handsonHtml/handson.html
http://www.python.org/dev/peps/pep-0008/
http://docs.python.org/2/library/subprocess.html
http://docs.python.org/2/tutorial/errors.html
http://docs.python.org/2/library/stdtypes.html
http://zetcode.com/lang/python/datatypes/

http://www.ibm.com/developerworks/library/os-python1/
http://pguides.net/python-tutorial/python-string-methods/
http://mkaz.com/solog/python-string-format
http://infohost.nmt.edu/tcc/help/pubs/python/web/old-str-format.html
http://www.tutorialspoint.com/python/python_strings.htm
http://docs.python.org/2/library/string.html
http://docs.python.org/2/library/queue.html
http://www.blog.pythonlibrary.org/2012/08/01/python-concurrency-an-example-of-a-queue/
http://stackoverflow.com/questions/2846653/python-multithreading-for-dummies
http://www.tutorialspoint.com/python/python_multithreading.htm
http://docs.python.org/2/library/time.html

Tkinter

http://effbot.org/tkinterbook/grid.htm
http://infohost.nmt.edu/tcc/help/pubs/tkinter/web/index.html
http://www.tkdocs.com/tutorial/windows.html
http://pages.cpsc.ucalgary.ca/~saul/personal/archives/Tcl-Tk_stuff/tcl_examples/
http://effbot.org/tkinterbook/
http://www.pythonware.com/library/tkinter/introduction/hello-tkinter.htm
http://www.tutorialspoint.com/python/python_gui_programming.htm
http://www.beedub.com/book/2nd/TKINTRO.doc.html
http://zetcode.com/gui/tkinter/menustoolbars/
http://effbot.org/tkinterbook/menu.htm
http://infohost.nmt.edu/tcc/help/pubs/tkinter/web/menu.html
http://www.tutorialspoint.com/python/tk_messagebox.htm
http://effbot.org/tkinterbook/canvas.htm
http://www.tutorialspoint.com/python/tk_canvas.htm

Linux

http://steve-parker.org/sh/intro.shtml

http://linuxtutorial.info/modules.php?name=MContent&pageid=329

http://en.wikibooks.org/wiki/Linux_For_Newbies/Command_Line

CPSIA information can be obtained at www.ICGtesting.com
Printed in the USA
LVOW03s1807041214

417200LV00022B/849/P